THE PACIFIC NORTHWEST POETRY SERIES

Linda Bierds, General Editor

THE PACIFIC NORTHWEST POETRY SERIES

the grief of a
happy life

CHRISTOPHER
HOWELL

UNIVERSITY OF WASHINGTON PRESS

Seattle

The Grief of a Happy Life, the twentieth volume in the Pacific Northwest Poetry Series, was published with the generous support of Cynthia Lovelace Sears.

This book was also made possible by gifts from Diane Crummett, Lynn Hays, and Nancy Nordhoff, in memory of Joseph Goldberg.

Design by Katrina Noble
Composed in Scala, typeface designed by Martin Majoor

23 22 21 20 19   5 4 3 2 1
Printed and bound in the United States of America

UNIVERSITY OF WASHINGTON PRESS
uwapress.uw.edu

JACKET DESIGN: Katrina Noble
JACKET ILLUSTRATION: Victoria Adams, *Lowlands #16*, encaustic on panel. Private collection, www.victoriaadamsart.com. Used by permission.

LIBRARY OF CONGRESS CATALOGING-IN-PUBLICATION DATA ON FILE
LC record available at https://lccn.loc.gov/2019018119

ISBN 978-0-295-74616-6 (hardcover)
ISBN 978-0-295-74615-9 (ebook)

The paper used in this publication is acid free and meets the minimum requirements of American National Standard for Information Sciences—Permanence of Paper for Printed Library Materials, ANSI Z39.48–1984.∞

for Barbara Ellen Anderson, spirit of my days

CONTENTS

III. ROADS, CROSSINGS & RETURNS

IV. EXALTATIONS

OUR PRAYERS ARE ANSWERED

—for the boys in the Shakespeare Club

In the café six of us
lean above our bowls
as if to read in them
a particularly fascinating
obituary

or the name of that
cad from sixth grade
who stole bicycle seats.

"Is there a heaven
of bicycle seats?"
does not occur to us.

Trucks go by.

We dream momentarily
of lovers in another time
meeting in cafés,
hiding out from the rain,

though we know

it is falling now again
and differently.

With small misshapen spoons
we tap on the edges
of our bowls,

finger the plastic flowers.

Six of us, waitress
like an angel of steam
waiting in the wings.

THE GRIEF OF A HAPPY LIFE

I.

BEACH GLASS

Our soul and body hold each other
tenderly in their arms like Charles Lamb
and his sister walking again to the madhouse.
Hand in hand, tears on their faces, him carrying
her suitcase.

—JACK GILBERT

THEOLOGIA

I. BEYOND THEOLOGY THE SOUL

walks out into morning's mists and roses
and huge dreaming sycamores
and slips a robe of leaves over its bony shoulders, as if
    to trade

some of its solitude for a little warmth, a little bit of the old earth
that has forgotten it.
When a fire truck rushes by on the way to a catastrophe,
    the soul bows

and enters the useless dance of sympathy, remembering Rome,
Chicago, the great blaze at Herculaneum.
When small birds mistake it for a tree, it makes the exhausted
    north wind sound

and takes them in and feeds them those tiny seeds the dry
leaves have hoarded all winter in their broken skin
as though they were children, their faces peering into the snow
    from dark windows

as the moon goes by and the clouds pass like centuries of houses
and roads and great armies whose souls are dented rust
and who, therefore, brim with sorrows and have only
    themselves to blame.

Crickets and katydids carve in air the soul's unlisted number
and the shapes it might, in a rush of joy, assume,
paying forward what the bent coin of flesh cannot afford
    to know: we are the guest

within us, always, that we be not without habitude or solace,
that we be not only what we have done and failed to do.

2. OPEN ANY DOOR

Sometimes I listen, then say one thing
then another to the first lifting eyelid
of the day, and put on my oldest shirt,
for the softness, and step out
and stand beside the hydrangea
with my cat just as the birds begin
their call and response.

The meaning of this eludes me, and my cat
makes no remark. We both look around
as though we had come here suddenly
from another world
nearby and so like this world
only a strangely velvet love of flowers
tells me I'm somewhere else.

We breathe deeply and consider
that some of those we love
may be already here, just beyond
the corner of the house
where someone exactly like my wife
has planted a perfect replica
of our sunset maple
so that coming here like this
we will not be frightened or put out
of reckoning by what is missing
or by the appearance
of what we had thought never
to see again.

So much may be near us now, we open
any door and take the sun in our mouths
and stroll into the huge meadow
we always knew was there
where the various gods, arms
heavy with grapes, laze
and bicker and agree
all afternoon.

3. KNOWLEDGE

It was not that we hated the snakes
necessarily, it was their movement
sent shivers into our shirtsleeves
like night dreads or the thought
of a car door closing on your thumb.
So we hoisted the unimaginably heavy
cinder blocks and let them fall
like the whole sky
onto their skinny heads.

Green stuff came out and they curled
like springs. It was a thing
we did in summer dust
as insects whirred and crackled
in the Johnson grass and vetch.

We called it forgiving the snakes,
confused as we were
about Eve, apples,
the Devil, and that "blood" our parents
drank in church, somber as we were
as we dug the secret graves
and fashioned the little crosses
that signaled the serpents' certain return
to grace. We did not know

what names to place there.
We looked up at the huge sky
out of which anything might fall
and, crying odd, inexplicable tears,
simply carved our own.

I think of the red umbrella
of the last god
hoping for rain
or fire or a see-through blouse
drifting in the moonlit trees.
I think of him filing his nails
with a miniature violin, its music
a scratch in the dark ice
of midnight cities
heaving in their wired sleep
and keeping up the payments.
I think of prayer and sacrifice
leaking like fireflies from his hair,
from the brittle ends
of his wings, if he has them, if he hasn't
pawned them feather by feather
like an echo eaten by the stones
or a promise lost in space.
Out of candles and out of luck,
I think he wonders
if this is already a kind of afterlife,
what's after that? Where
do the dead gods go
with their loneliness?
Would it help to be a woman
or a song?
I imagine useless juju flitting around him
like a whirlwind of confused birds
left out of the migration.

Surely, at last, he embraces
his empty sleeves and lets go,
as the Buddha must have, knowing that
even gods are only what they are
and that there is always more or less nothing
but to be
and begin again.

5. LACRIMAE RERUM

And they rent their garments
and painted their foreheads with ash
in supplication and lament.
The bright stone of the moon
bent down, still
upon the water where they stood
to the knees in cold, reflected stars.
Breeze in branches made the sound

of women wiping their eyes with paper
or breathing in an icy room.

Everyone knew the angel had died
fruitlessly for their sakes, for the tin
and frayed lace rations of joy safekept
still in their original wrappings and bows,
and for the tears of things, God's
equalizing measure, deep and dreaming,
shadowless as water, lonely
as a dance.

6. IN CONSEQUENCE

For hours we hid behind the false wall
Henrik had constructed in the barn
before he was caught and changed.
Hours of stiff silence, our breathing
soft as daisies in a bowl.
When at last the special detachment
gave up and moved on, firing the house
in a parting gesture of contempt, we loosened
the secret latch and stepped out, new born
among the dead.

Beyond asking why, we considered God's absence,
a notion evil in itself, we thought, finally,
and set out with three tins of soup, a blanket, two
loaves of black bread, and each other, damaged
but alive.

Moving by night, steadily
north, it was difficult to avoid the dogs
run wild in packs, the bounty hunters mad
to curry favor with the directorate
charged with mopping up.
Twice, by accident, we led one to the other
and escaped in the dust and screaming.

Through the endless days we hid
in caves and thickets, fighting off or eating
whatever else might live there.
Weeks of this. Luckily
our shoes held up, and patches of snow

could yet be found in shaded corners of the heights
to which we came at last. So we had water.

The rest is as I told you, we came in sight
of the border, dashed across, and so became
new, faith rising in us again, joyous and
broken, staring at its hands, folded, strangely
unable to pray.

7. PARADISE NULL

The road out is like the road in, crooked
with crooked little devils waving
at the edges as we pass.
We want just a small bite, they say, just a piece
of you for the collection plate,
in remembrance.

And in remembrance we carry the sodden
equations of memory
like children's clothes snatched off the line
as rain approached, twisting its blue-black hands.

Here's the one about the girl who wept
and said I didn't like her anymore when I didn't
even know who she was.

Here's my grandmother blinking in the dappled
orchard, her calm face, her apron heavy
with windfall apples. A bit
of traffic goes by on the dirt road.

If we're lucky, the angels
in which we have never believed descend
and select from the tatters a small article of faith.
But this road

does not double back. No one is given the beanstalk
magic by which to swarm into that Heaven
where the giant lives and lives.

Nearby, the angels laugh like rocks
sliding down a slope.

They shoot skeet (who needs devils?) in the Elysian fields,
    blasting
our loves and vanities into a golden spray, a few
lost feathers drifting down after.

Not the best sport
but it's what they have. Sometimes, I believe,
they wish God would wake and tell them what to do
(if there *is* anything to do)
about suffering, the grey heaps of it

beside the road, the pathetic singing
they almost hear as they light their huge cigars.

8. KIERKEGAARD'S INSTANT

I.

So simple, the fearlessness
and suffering and ignoring the doors
as they close.
Remember the word "forever"? built
of the hard, invisible bricks, forgotten suicides
in their white boaters and cheap rings?
Who could love this life again, knowing
what it meant
and who could not?
God is a walkingstick of bones broken
into song the long roads embrace, loving
that taste of dust, their brother.

Grieve for joy, if you must
pray. Or
dance for grief.

II.

The telephone is ringing
and it's St. Paul, again, the operator, bishop
of limited offers, martyr of the party line.
He says, "I'm sorry, sir, the number
you are not calling is your own forgotten
name.
Please deposit whatever may pass for praise
and every half-invented memory of joy, just
for the record.
This has been a recorded massage."

III.

Look inward, are those the dead lakes
in which the spirit swims, nursing
its prosthetic smile? Overgrown gardens
on the shore are thick with violet-blue
birds; and the trees are everyone
you have ever loved, even for a moment,
that single moment we have.

9. DARK NIGHT: NEWPORT, 4:00 A.M.

The lighthouse lamp goes starry and goes dark.
The sea will not forbid itself the shore.
Listen, you can hear the Dog Star bark
Louder than it ever barked before.

You lie awake and count yourself again
And find that more is less and less is more.
Where you are is where you've always been.
The sea will not forbid itself the shore.

What loneliness compels you to arise
And touch the broken edges of the dark?
Is it greater than the loneliness of skies?
Listen, you can hear the Dog Star bark

Louder than it ever barked before.
Your life falls into blackness like a spark.
The sea will not forbid itself the shore.
The lighthouse lamp goes starry and goes dark.

I have begun to think that God is small
like a wren, a piece of blue
beach glass
shining in the wet
of sea and sky, that double exposure. Every day

the huge sun, the blue vault brimming
with invisible stars.
Each night the echoing expanse
of dark and always God in the palm of my hand,
fluttering, gleaming like the soul

with sweetness, with a vast
reluctance to change us or give us
anything but that sweetness, dismissed
by the world
because it is so small.

II.

HISTORICAL PERSPECTIVE

I wakened
read the paper

and thought of you one by one
and tried to hold your faces
in my eyes

—PHILIP LEVINE

HISTORICAL PERSPECTIVE

Blue spider mincing along the spine
of my tattered volume of Tacitus, if you are
the ghost of Professor Schnackenberg

who caused me to acquire the book, how is it
to walk as though made of glass
conjecture? I'll bet

it's hard to fold up those legs when
not in use,
when you're dreaming of your old

fireside, surrounded by beautiful
daughters who fail to believe you
will ever die. I failed to believe it also, and

here you are! terribly changed but still
contentious, eyes sparking like fists
of tiny diamonds, beginning to weave

what will become your other
history. When once in a while your old name
comes up, I, ghostly student,

will shake my head, "Ah, Tacitus. Contention
and change, always his special topics."
Tacitus, who became this book

in which I find you again.

CREATION

Aeneas, who never existed, suddenly ignites
among the statuary in a Roman garden.
In his hand is an astrolabe
carved from the shell of something extinct.
His shoes are made of opals
and, when he isn't listening, they speak of something
they keep calling "science." So what? perhaps, but
since this is fiction, anything might happen
and you can see by his tremulous hands
that Aeneas knows this. He knows, also,
that small Trojan horses suddenly surround him,
can hear the tiny heroes they contain laughing
and singing that obscene song about Helen
"spreading her wings." And while that's going on
a jetliner flies over, silently,
as though Aeneas and all the world is roofed
by an enormous glass-topped table.
If he looks hard, he can see faces of the muses
etched into its atmosphere among images
of lyres and grapes and strange
contraptions with wheels on every side.
Poor Aeneas who never asked for this,
who has no friends but Dido up-in-smoke,
who has been jerked into being, handed
a pound of nails and six twelve-foot staves

and nothing to do but to construct whatever joy
or nonsense the subtle mind might make of them.
Meanwhile in a secret scriptorium someone illumines
that kind of dream we call a story
and slathers it over Aeneas as he wakes inside its basic idea.
Oh precious precious life, it is, yes, that
story, and though it is so small a moment, even
Aeneas swells with the glory
of its impossible grace.

EARLY POEM UPON MY FATHER'S BIRTHDAY SIXTEEN YEARS AFTER HIS DEATH

Through the window at first light comes
first light
filled with the shuffling fat raccoon and its six kits
bound for the great good grace
of the compost heap. Nothing so bright
as their eyes
spilling whatever sun there is, nothing so hazily curious
as my face, wreathed in steam from my coffee,
hair and beard still disordered by sleep.

The moon is down.
Ice glitters on the flat stone path.
In my dream last night I went back to sea
alone
on a ship of grey voices that would not speak.

Because my name and my father's name were lost,
I wept.
Something handed me a note that read,
Wake up!
every name is lost.

Suddenly seven raccoons were standing
in a great cold sunlit room
watching me sleep.

GRAHAM GREENE

It is the hour of weeping women, public and somehow
    unselfconscious,
as though they believe mourning has made them silent and
    invisible.

In the cobbled courtyard a young cavalry officer raises his
    sword
six paces left of the firing squad, the condemned man
    whistling

as a bird goes past a half-deaf painter in a straw hat sketching
    quickly
just that moment. Perhaps it is this to which the weeping
    refers.

Perhaps it is for a taxi lost in the smoke of a collapsed
    building, basket of fruit
and a child waiting forever now (curious phrase) in the back
    seat. Perhaps

the scratched wall of a dungeon is the problem, or sunlight's
    refusing to be
that shade of gold forgetfulness the painter will work lovingly
    into his depiction

of law and folly, the angles and separate elements composing
    themselves
like all the sorrows that, though actual, cannot be explained.

A DOLL'S HOUSE

What if the doll comes alive
and blames you
because you are a god to it
and have knowledge
of before the doll awoke with a vile
suddenness in the attic under a pile
of old clothes, its grinning cry
announcing a shift in the usual order
of displacements, in even the crenellations
in the castle wall, if there has been a castle,
if it had a name like Stonerose Keep
or the Palace of Bonefleet, where a small girl
once set out her toy tea things and gave the doll
a magic sip and now the doll has remembered this
one fragment of its past and is wondering
when the girl might return, the girl
who is mad in the attic and slowly
shredding her life story with
curled yellow fingernails, dressing herself
in a little apron and a little smile, her eyes
opening and closing opening and closing as she
grinds a blue-white substance to finer
and finer powder, wondering where
has the prince got to and will it
ever again be time
for tea?

SOMEWHERE BEHIND THE BLANK SCREENS

the gunslingers of my youth
wake up cold, fires smoked away
into the chill trees, horses gone
leaping the moon like nursery rhyme cows.
In the underbrush
ghostly theme songs trouble the dry sticks
and Butch Cavendish cleans his guns.
Nothing else to be done.

Red Rider and Maverick and Paladin have to know
they have been alone like this
for decades, that even the reruns are archeological
oddities headed for a vault
somewhere, that the Rifleman and Cheyenne
have ridden off over a hill
fifty years from where the rancher's daughter waits
and waits. Who was that masked man, anyway,

Cisco? In another clearing
far from where the aging sheriff dreams
by his stove, the rugged drifter with no name
counts his few remaining lucky stars, their tired
glimmer like eyes he imagines
watching from the dark
future of his loneliness, the desert
of his deadly and beautiful heart.

A SO-CALLED RESPITE

I.

The Portuguese taxi driver said, "Sailor,
Paolo knows just
what you want: a woman
who will screw your nuts off
for just fifty escudos."
I said it sounded painful, and he said
that all the great pleasures
were painful, that life itself would be nothing
if not for its beautiful pain.
I said, "Yes, I think that's so.
But I'd just as soon keep my nuts."

II.

It was Lisbon, 1969, and considering
what was going on in Asia, it was great
to have a European cruise
just at that time. But, in some ways,
it might as well have been Rome
in the time of the Republic
when, after years on the ramparts in Gaul,
the legionnaires were granted extended leave
and all indiscretions short of murder
were ignored.

III.

The driver let me out at a place called
the Texas Bar in the alley next to which
a sailor was beating a marine over the head
with a wicker-bound wine bottle.

Inside, a three-piece combo, featuring
an accordion, a tuba, and a flute,
entertained the drunken minions of the NATO fleet
with "Hey, Jude." A naked woman danced
like a zombie on the bar.

IV.

Buffeted in the crush of reveling men
and incredibly friendly women, I spilled my beer
on a boatswain and he jumped up,
marched me outside
and pasted me a good one.
I slugged him back, and we both stood there
bleeding. I thought about the Mekong and the armies
making the same history we were making
right there. I thought about pain,
and the boatswain bought me another beer.

V.

Somewhere around 1200 BC, Priam
looking out over the plains of Troy
saw that true sorrow is the end of worlds,
that pain is how you know the end
has not found you, that something remains
and you are its soldier.

CANTICLE OF GILGAMESH
RETURNED FROM HEAVEN

As Enkidu came down from the mountain so
the sky accepts us
whichever way we fall. New sky will spread its tresses,
a known and not known truth, as the beasts
know nothing of our names.
Enkidu was the name of a man of ripe pears.
One life will lay no finger to his dancing.
It may step and turn all its days at the gate
and not pass through this truth
without wings and nothing for a brother and no one
for a soul except the one life's locket with its secret
key of grass. Shocking that the one life comes only
once, Enkidu, beautiful brother who drinks of the heart's
dark water, who takes amber for his meat
and is a lamp to which the one life turns as to the sun,
though, as to the sun, who can say
the truth of that almost mortal fire so long and bright.
Forgive me, I am nothing like the king
or the king's messenger.
I am the one without plight or vengeance, Enkidu,
I am the one question walking
the one path.

BEFORE GENESIS

1.

We rose at dawn, struggled into our clothes,
drifted down to the gravel lot
in front of Jespersen's Big Little Store, and stood
clutching our lunch sacks and yawning
like a gaggle of pink-faced angels waiting for the bus
that would bring us out the gates
of our pearlescent lives and into the province
of a loud-voiced man who would assign us rows
by the careful and utter harvesting of which
we might redeem him

and ourselves as well, depending.

2.

In the beginning the chill of the dew-heavy leaves
was a penance hard to bear. Yet
we strapped on the little breadbox carriers
and plunged our hands in among the stiff canes
with their offerings of berries, pendulous, bumping
as we troubled the greenery, our movements swift
and raggedly precise. And at row's end, of course,
we would cross over and go back
as we had come.

3.

Soft thud
of fruit falling into hallocks.
Chatter and whoop of the birds.
Mr. Derschmidt yelling at his enormous wife,
"Them rows was all done yesterday,
Eunice!"

4.

A few large spiders and once in a while
a harmless snake. Sun
high and hot by ten, the shirts come off
and the second hundred years of the day
begins. Lunch
approaches with infinitesimal slowness, one island
moving toward another, as we labor to be fruitful, to multiply
the sum of earth's blessings and earn enough
to know what we deserve.

5.

The lunch hour passes like the hour
before an execution, though the last meal is beautiful,
sprawling in shade by the barn,
warm grass beneath us and an immense blue
diamond that goes on and on
above.

6.

That girl, the serious girl with violet
eyes, falls asleep under the great
maple

and when Derschmidt starts yelling again
that "Berries don't pick themselves!" I am the one
who somehow dares to touch her shoulder
and say, "He's calling. We've got to go back."

Heaven was like that.

IMPLICIT

Simply the last one
writes in gold on a pale
blue cheekbone of sky
above a hill.
Gaunt cows in a field
go on forgetting,
their curiosity twitching
on and off
like a series of casual maimings:
beheaded garter snakes, heaps
of wingless bees, the sweet
neighborhood children
thinking of lunch as they work.
Could it be the last one,
a chime
of the not and never?
There it goes, fading now,
and we can't stop its going.
Should we
hold hands, perhaps
sing? Offer all we have
if only? Is it so
important, really? When
you think about it
who cares if it's the last one, just

like each of us
becoming rumor
of an absent mist, light of a long
dead star
in our future past?
Who cares but our barren
and angry sister, the earth,
remembering plenitude.

THE LAST BUS

I stood on desolate Pacific Avenue, waiting for the last bus to Parkland, though it would go only as far as D Street and turn back to the barn, leaving me to trudge like a fallen angel past the strip clubs, bars, and all-night diners, past the loom of last call and drowsy cabbies eyeing me blankly, Patsy Cline and Connie Francis leaking from their radios like all the sorrow in the world.

I had been to see my girl, spent the week's six bucks on bus fare, the movie, coffee, and had just enough left to get me almost home. Maybe I thought of the tower room above the Music Department where we made love in a splash of the moon. Maybe I thought such nights would never end, that love would be the food that would nourish wonder all the way to God.

It began to rain. Maybe I knew we would become strangers as I was myself a kind of stranger. The crooked neon smile on the sign of the Silver Slipper said this was likely. Maybe I thought of the two cigarettes waiting in my room next to a history of the Roman republic, glorious, righteous, and doomed by nothing but the world it had itself assembled, believing it would last as the gods would last.

Maybe the boy I was thought this terrible or mysterious or right as the rain that made him shiver and wonder who he was and if true destiny was, perhaps, the mirrored shape of all that would never be. I have walked ever since with the weight of the obvious growing less and love, singular, lit from within as though it were a house or that last bus parked somewhere, out beyond the rain.

HOME ON THE RANGE; OR, MORTALITY
AND THE PERSISTENT FAILURE TO ARRIVE

Spitting snow. A ring on the eyelid
of a lizard afraid to sleep.
And then, of course, wind
grinding the flakes to a grit marbled
absence of solace.
Those ducks
hunching by the shore cannot know
who shot at and missed them, or why
each moment betrays the one before
in payment so perfect, even the lizard shies
out of its way and the wind's voice
stops and starts
as though speaking of this by a grey shed
in north-central Wyoming
where the deer and the antelope play only
in memory.
And beyond memory a stranger
fails to arrive, though we have waited
like mourners at an empty grave
all the livelong day
and wolves gather in the hills.

OVID STILL

Publius Ovidius Naso, exiled for his cheek,
wrote Caesar Augustus
every day for years to apologize
and to beg. I see him now in the corner
of a café on Third Street, mumbling as he bends
above yellowed sheets of foolscap
with his nub of a pencil.
His torn and smelly tunic looks like roses
runover by a rainfall of disasters and his hair
is the color of outhouse mold.
If he remembers the crowds and the cheering
outside the temple of Venus, if he has spent
the night at the Brothers of Merciful Communion
Mission, he hasn't told Caesar or anyone
like Caesar. But he's telling the crows
now, the three scratching his name
on their shadows and calling him Clyde,
the three he has drawn on a yellow sheet,
balled up and smoothed out and balled up
again, like regret.

Oh dearest Master, two thousand years gone
among the Elysians, he writes,
lettest thou thy servant return in peace.
Forgivest thou his fuckups for the love of God

or his own meager grace so infinitely less magnificent
than thine, oh ruler of all lands and seas, master
of even the very air and the fiery daemons there of!

Then he rises, to ease that wound in his back
from a recent stabbing, and thinks of boxcars
and smoke and cops coming out of the wall
like Caesar's agents of Imperial Security
brandishing their copper-bound saps, driving
the riffraff away from the steps of the Forum,
dragging them off the train. And it's confusing;
I can see his disappointment broken into
hexametric couplets shining like neon
in his dirty spectacles as he shakes his head
to clear it and to scatter the crows
that are laughing again, with a sound
like blackboards eating themselves with the truth
about metamorphosis, that it goes where it wants,
like a river, once you let it loose, Ovid, old boy
in the pink Value Village shoes and ruined face,
poet of lost life begging every Caesar to give him
one more chance to change into a man
who can come home, even if home is nothing
but a name
written in want and dust.

GOD BLESS THE CHILD

I think of the sax man in Copenhagen:
a little freebasing before the concert,
some slow breathing under the high notes
and a woman languorous and desiring
as he touches or thinks of her
lightly. No
trickery to it.
No satin sheets or sudden cold air
out along the canal of his imagination
as he turns out lights
in the greenroom
and climbs the stairs like someone else
that night. A good night,
all in all, the weather of time
loving it, sax like the woman's nipple
responding, if it did
so that flesh enters the music from offstage,
making a window of it and outside
the leaves spiral back up
onto the trees. Come on, sweet
mama, we're going to be dead
a long time
is what his lips are saying as the audience
sways and he is miles and miles
away, lonely for everything he has.

III.

ROADS, CROSSINGS & RETURNS

I imagine that these thousand
sleek, invisible zebras are
leading me somewhere;

it is the moment before
birth, I expect, and follow.

—JAMES TATE

SAINT THERESA RETURNS

She came back
unremarked
in that out-of-the-way town
until she was seen
to be weeping

and it went on and on, her weeping, soft
as the voice of sleep, which
many ignored, though the birds
ceased their chatter
and inclined their heads as if
to listen.

At the crofter's hut where she came,
at last, to live, she sat for hours
by the iron stove and, when the fire
went out, sat there still
as a stone in a stream
and wept.

No help emerged from sun or shadow
or the neighborhood with its considerate
paths and gardens. Everything
seemed to be thinking
of itself, and so
her solitude was all she had, that

and the weeping, which she also possessed
entirely.

Was there a grave involved, blood?
Was she seeking refuge
from a country overrun, leaving all behind
among the lost children with their somber
and enormous eyes?

Perhaps she was inhuman, like hatred or snow
or the ghost of a hammer
rusting in grass beside a disused road.
Was her heart a flaming arrow of columbine
or rue,
the blossoming of which her tears sought
to obviate?

Perhaps on the far side of universal flux
changelessness defies all calculus and mirth
by existing as a possibility and weeping was her form
of understanding this.

Seasons erected and dispelled themselves.
Armies entered the swim of violence,
wearing sacrifice and honor like name tags
or artificial wings edged in red. Fire became

conscious. It was the new
new world we have,

and soon all the saints were weeping.

THE END OF HERACLEITUS

The next thing was a path beside the water
and what the crows saw there
in full aching bloom.
These were followed by mouths in flight
above the city with its blue flash
of windows and what someone thought
of that. Then there was that forsakenness
and pride of those who had found the path
and water joined in a fluxion of promise,
becoming, and winding away. At last
came the men of flowers
and wind stirring them and women
in their millions
begging for joy, cracking its shells
with their teeth.

SEASONS OF LOVE AND WATER

I.

The rain came every day, like a dreaming horse
returning to the barn. It had about it the warmth
of cold, that special endlessness
pooling and playful when we turned away, forgetting
to complain.

At night in our beds we heard the rain's voices
on windows and the ghosts of vanished leaves.

In the morning the rain would be there still, a curtain
of beads the grey-blue color of ice
through which red barns, and sheds blackened by sleep,
looked back at us.

II.

Hardly a man knew me, dragging my flails and signal flags,
hoping open tunnels in the ryegrass, gulls
tilting above.

Shall I explain my feet to you, widen my eyes
as I smile? What if the horse never
comes home, if we mint ourselves again
and turn up dead?

Even God thinks these things
when it's raining, though I am sorry to have said that.

III.

Oh, I don't know. The cherries were in bloom, the calm
harbor asleep with its boats. Who cared, really, about the rain?
The way she sat on the edge of the bed and looked at him,
    clearly
she would be leaving soon.

No wind at all that day. Irises in a pink bowl. I don't know.
He touched her and thought he would die of it.

In another world, the world of prospective memory, she would
    reopen
like an iris. And now, again, he is afraid to think of her.

SIMPLE OPERATION

I.

The incision was not precise,
as if, in the last blaze
of summer flowers the young girls
had tucked away like secrets,
some of the horses had escaped
their riders, paddocks, and barns.
It was next to nothing, that condition
and no one but the surgeon knowing it
with his gloved fingertips.
It was almost the only thing
left when the dreaming turned
to question something the King's
fool had whispered, just as the tall
trees whisper, not meaning to.
And when they removed
the rest of him, the sighing remained,
a blue-textured singe
as if shadows of the horses and forgotten friends,
a currency, had come into his lake-like eyes
and outside it was snowing.

II.

The universe opens its enormous mouth
and the world enters, one life at a time.
Yet something endures and we
are its metaphor. Broken, repaired
and filled with love
we rise again. These are our last words
to each other as the gurney disappears
down the hall.

GLIMPSED IN PASSING

Owls glide
back into the trees.
There goes the milkman
with his jingling bottles,
dust pursuing him
down the bumpy road.

Blackbirds in a willow,
robins in the grass. All of it
years ago or infinite
as a moment painted on a wall
and the wall itself forgotten.

Ten thousand years, half a million
ghost lights on a hillside
in a water ball of glass,
in the arch of a thumbnail, brow
of a beautiful face
glimpsed in passing.

BETWEEN SHORES

I. ANOTHER CROSSING

It was the river of death
and we crossed it
or the river of forgetting
which is why I don't remember
crossing it,
holding your hand as we were reborn
strangers to every river
and ourselves, fly away spirits
whose bodies were dreaming.
Love was not our number
and the days, if they were days,
were like any dark limb or whistle,
any momentary singing
from the back room of an old hotel
where no one sat at the bar
with no one else
carving in dust the signals
of our disappearance.
What is a wound if not this
crossing under the moonlike eyes
of the boatman who has waited
among the willows

all these years, sad king of patience,
old blue fire of human things,
last things, beauty itself
bent to its oars inside us.

2. TO GET ANYWHERE

—for James Tate

Jesus sat down in the dust.
"Well," he said, "the body must walk a long way
in this life."
He said this to no one, but meant it
anyway.

After awhile some men came out of the bushes
and asked what the hell he was doing there.
Jesus! Didn't he know this was private property?

Well, Jesus got up, slowly, and blessed them
before moving on, stopping every few yards to scrawl
in charcoal on a wall or tree or rock:

"Should a peaceful life really require this much kindness?"
    or
"Jews are my best friends. I myself am a Jew.
Later this will be conveniently forgotten. Trust me."
    or
"The dust is beautiful. See how it rises and falls to rise again
again."

As he plodded on he kept thinking, "I wish
I had a donkey. With a donkey you don't have to
walk, you can go anywhere. There'd be no stopping me
if I had a donkey."

3. INGMAR BERGMAN POSTCARD

Craze-green dragonflies French
kiss that tense river
over which the old are passing
in boats made of moldy leaves.

How much *time* it takes
to know one's life
has found its edge, to understand
to whom the boatman's sorrow
again and again belongs.

The bravest leap out and swim for it,
forgetting stroke by stroke which
shore is for candles and which
for stones.

As Dante crossed the Lethe
he thought, "I'm on the wrong
boat!" and, outraged, "Look how *wide!*
Must be the wrong river, too!"
But after three or four weeks
there seemed nothing for it
and he settled down with a hunk
of cheese and a crossword,
occasionally asking the Florentine
hatter on his left how he might
spell "Dalmatian" or "fruititarianism"
or "bloviate," and hoping that,
if the weather turned rough,
he wouldn't vomit on anyone's
shoes.

It was 1321. The sky was
marbled pewter and filled with
white birds as the boat was filled
with the sadness of departure,
which had been sudden, in most
cases, so that faces of the left behind
could yet be seen
shining in the eyes of the dead;
another thing Dante had not expected.

Every ten minutes the boatman
stopped rowing and demanded
more money, knowing his passengers
had already lost everything they had.

Then he would roar and stomp
at the perfection of his joke, tears
of ecstatic amusement cascading
into his beard. "What a jerk,"
Dante thought. "Must we really
supply *all* the dignity here?"

He vowed to take this up
with whomever might prove prince
of that nether shore,
still oddly distant and dark blue
as a fine cloak
he had once seen Brunetto Latini fling
for no reason onto the shoulders
of an old woman
bent under a load of onions.

Ah, well, the world was a mystery.
And where was Brunetto now
and where was the woman?
Where was Beatrice? come
to think of it.
Were their rivers as wide
and lonely as his? And how
do you spell "eidetic" he asked,
"I keep forgetting."

5. MESSAGE

She had come down the lane
and was like the lane
itself, a narrow kind of edge
among life's greenery
as we said then.
I knew her touch in the dark
admirably soft almost
voice-like
as my face swam in her hair, immunized
against disaster and failing
to count change against cost, the trivial
against a wound so deep
the day turned suddenly to wonder what
gave God such a long head start.
When I put her aboard the night boat
a last time,
my sighs kept dividing
each thought of her from the independent
countries
of that error.
Not that I would cut myself over this
loss.
Not that she didn't turn and look back
at a cloud drifting to pieces above me
like a message torn and flung
against the wind, the drift of it for once
readable, its result going on
and on like a life
sentence or a mortgage, or a ship that departs

one night
and forgets the port it was bound for,
the land it left behind, and whoever
might have been happy there.

6. UNDERWAY

—for James Oscar Johnsrud: in memoriam

The old men rise, walk down
to the quiet inlet
and climb carefully into their boats.

They stretch their backs still stiff from sleep.
They study the sky for signs of storm
before placing the thole pins and oars, shoving off
into the pre-morning stillness. Eventually, they know,
there will be wind and wave.
But, so what? Their boats, built with a lifetime
of care, are well-found, beautiful
in their way
and it is wonderful to suppose them indestructible
as dreams that might contain every happiness and mistake,
every little piece of light that lent its reasons
to time.

The old men are far from shore now, leaning
into their task, calm as the last stars
that are just winking
out.

TURNPIKE AND FLOW

I.

We say it is a long road
but it is only
a life
slipping past, dark and bright, abandoning
a few broken tools and shoes, once
in a while something beautiful but too big
to carry. Of course, nothing but the road
can make it the whole way.

II.

Every day I think you will return to me
who has kept faith
in the dark and slobber of the body's wish, in flint
of the crow's musing. Every day
I find I am the empty room we joked about
and always you are the absence
of a door.

III.

Listen. I am tapping another song
of grit and tin,
a hollow, forgotten, underplanetary voice
become again a mole's longing for the sun

he cannot deserve.
Forgive me, at last. I have come so far.
Here is my payment of sticks, the shivering
charm of my passage.

WORDSWORTH

I.

Light snow on the hills
and cornstalks like the grizzled
dilapidated hair of old men on benches
outside the dispensary
where they have been waiting six hundred years
for dawn.

II.

The dead stay where they are,
though all night there may have been
some question
because of the dark wistfulness
of the living.
Because of the unnamed sounds
of sorrow
leaping out of dreams
with nowhere to go after the bars close.
Because of still lakes in the mind
to which nothing but the mind returns.

III.

I was cloud-like and lonely?
When the singing stopped

I wandered out of myself
to tell you this, to give myself
the abstract pleasure
of handing out flowers, daffodils
it turns out.

THE BETTER PART OF VALOR

My newly divorced neighbor leaves at eight
in his shining SUV, his bald head newly polished,
happy smirk decorating his face like steel wool
on a birthday cake. Moments later
his ex drives up in her faded Ford Escort.
She hurries to the door and hammers so hard
you could hear it two blocks away.
Of course, no one answers
and you can tell by her posture she's sorry
to have done this, and pissed off at herself
and everybody else to have been caught doing it.
Stupidly, I wave
and she flips me off as she jogs, red-faced
to the car, which, of course, grinds and coughs
and fails to start. When I walk over
to see if I can help, her face is swollen
and wet with the tears and mucus of real rage.
When I tap on the window, she locks the doors
and beats her head against the steering wheel,
accidentally engaging the horn, which blasts
and blasts in joyously unrelieved malfunction.

Soon other neighbors, startled away
from their TVs, are running toward the commotion,
and the woman in the car is screaming

and tearing her hair.
So I call the fire department
and they're there in seconds, sirens blaring,
neighbors running around and around the car,
one guy trying to open the hood to get at the wiring
of the horn, a fireman in full battle gear approaching
with an axe.

Just then the former husband returns, his new
girlfriend draped all over him. "Oh boy, this is
great!" says Terry Dixon, the plumber
who lives two houses down. Someone else speculates
that the woman may try to kill herself; after all, *he* would.

But she's quiet now, her face perfectly composed.
She looks at the house that was her home for so many years
then up through the windshield at the bluish moon
as though it has said something profoundly predictable
and tries the ignition again.
The car starts.
The horn stops its screaming, and she drives away
leaving us all staring at each other, at the vaguely
flummoxed firemen, at our own houses
that seem suddenly fragile, quiet
and wrong.

IT'S DIFFICULT TO MEAN ONE'S WORDS

I said, "Hold me,"
and you heard, "Give me your life," and maybe
it was true I meant the sky was far too
large to bear alone.
I said, "Forgive me," and you heard, "Once again all must be
permitted."
But what did I mean?

It's so lonely, not knowing
one's words, their destinations like moving trains
far out on the dark prairie, lights flickering as they twist
among the gullies and hills, the long moan
of them announcing the Doppler distortions between
thought and sound, the clatter
of syllables rushing toward something blind and struggling,
tied to the rails.

END

—for Robert Abel: in memoriam

The path behind us marks
            our turns
and line of fall. Maps
rain clouds all
            momentary exaltations
come to earth. Why not
choose the stars?
        After all
huddled by fires singing or
dancing we have bent to them
            the names
of gods
    and the seers of Trismegistus
found there
    a mirroring
window
between fate and will. In the end
                still
it is earth: dust to dust
            dust to love
and be free of love

dust to murder
>>dust to justice
dust to rose
>>and the end
with our hands of smoke
our faces gone to rain
>>>>the dream life
burning out.
Such sweetness in the breast is
>>>>our only
home
>>finally
where we know ourselves beyond
>>reason
>>>with its riot gear
>>>its metal birds and clocks and disquisitions
beyond despair and triumph
>>>>and their masks gazing
>>>>>eternally back.
Such sweetness in completion
>>>>joining again
what was broken
>>>>the path itself healing
itself
as it goes.

IV.

EXALTATIONS

God, you're still so rich today!
Can I be you or live in your attic.
I see your house in my face.
We could both use another smile, less thinking.

—RAY AMOROSI

AS HE IS

After years of study, intense
penetration of the unknown continents
of his nature and of the world's tippy
and mysterious balance between
the dialects of love and loss,
he began to hope he might say something
wise.

He stared into the storm-darkened
atmospheres of the past and found a face
exhausted by the job of staring back.
He mixed some historical perspective
with a few photographs, various rubrics,
and discovered his friends and the women
he had loved earnestly discussing his failures,
how they were the principal failures
of everyone since Gilgamesh, how he simply
couldn't be blamed, personally; after all,
he was only a man—as if, with a little effort,
he might have been something else.

Their words filled him with weary affection
and he breathed deeply of the epiphanal
realization
that wisdom does not inhere in the mind, exactly,

but in experience, and that it was his task
to arrive again and again
at this Sisyphean terminus, this fallen
and refallen leaf.

It was very late.
He lit a small fire in a bowl,
looked out at the rain
and wrote this.

WINTER COMPANION

When I step outside, February air is chopped ice chandeliers
circling themselves in a barn so huge
the birds are actually uncertain and with wild twitterings
    inquire,
"Which way to Louisville? Is this Baja?"

And while that's going on, a transparent beast of light stalks
    among them,
turns left
at the end of that street where the old woman hates her yard,
    and howls away
toward the river.

Maybe I go back in and maybe I carry a candle out among the
    darkening
cottonwoods
where the deer, shaggy in their winter jackets, hold mute
    convocation.
Maybe I whisper a little.

It all depends, I tell myself, hands shaping the distance
    between shrugging
and that waitress
all those years ago who pitied my hapless face and stepped out
    of her uniform
to warm my bones.

If the sky is spitting snow, I keep moving my big old boots so
     when the wind
comes I'm busy
and far from that secret he's always trying to get me to reveal.
Fuck the wind.

These are my steps. That's my door. Inside and out, I am the
     world and the world
owns itself.
I say these things, offer my candle to the chill whether it
     remembers me
from the old days, whatever

they were, or is simply February's brainless child, breaking
     things because
that is what it does.
Maybe I remember to forgive its lack of mercy, or maybe,
     someplace else,
the fallen leaves

live on as pears and limes, or something indestructible, like
     hope.
How could I hope to know? I open
the door, I step outside. Maybe my whispers go up smokelike
     to the giant
ear of God, maybe not.

Which way to Louisville? Who owns this barn? What is the
     name of this
peaceful alarm?

CLOUD OF UNKNOWING

It is always the not known
I speak of, a kind of wandering,
looking for what I'm looking for, hearing it
over the next hill: band music
or the quiet of a crowd that might be there.
Like blind Tiresias I see
what I see without meaning to,
without payment and regretting only
myself for no reason, though reason
is my shadow and my shine.
[Sometimes I want you to stop
reading so I can
go on alone into the dark sublingual light
that rises from the dead, that perfection of being,
stars dizzy in the diastolic arabesque
of the universe, the inextinguishable music
in deaf Beethoven's head.]
Then I think, this is all about forgiveness.
Then I think this is all about not thinking
about breath
and then the snow
falling on cottonwoods along the river
and the sunlight afterward
and no one there.

THE GIANT CAUSES THE APOCALYPSE

He has lost the tiny set screw that keeps the world
taut, dropped it in the swamp,
fed it to the geese, forgot
it in a back room or the garden patch.

You may be sure an accounting will be called for
when the gods and demons finish
their bowling match.

Even the clueless sheriff will turn, puzzled,
in his chair as the hearts of huge stones crack
and beasts remember they were not always here.

Sage and thyme and the clock's ticktock
tack like spiders in midair.
The few small things that mattered are not there.

Jack and the beanstalk weep. But what will comfort *us*
as we hear our singing stop?
Love and light fade out
while the Giant stands among us lost in thought.

SURVEILLANCE

Don't leave the bear, either
frozen or shambling, unobserved.
You'll never know her children
in their red and blue boots, never guess
what the papa bear said to the pig
in that book of animals believing themselves
ennobled by restraint, swaying together
in tall reeds of a farmer's dream
or a hunter's wild shaking as he rushes
to lock and load and wake again
bereft.

Don't leave the bear
to others
who may fail to bear witness,
as they say, to her momentary genius
and the papa bear's soul like a drum.
It would be wrong, such absence
of ritual observation. Everything
must be seen
and after that there must be the dancing
and the weeping
and the feast.

THE BIOGRAPHICAL IMPERATIVE

I. WHEN WE WERE VERY YOUNG

How quiet it was
in the morning, you could hear
the dicky birds
and the way sun loosened the leaves
from their chill sleep,
could hear a raccoon climbing out
of the compost heap.
I thought I might hear even
the women sighing as they passed
on the dirt road down which
their husbands had disappeared
on their way to the Korean War.
"That's what they get for joining
the reserves," my uncle said
as some of the neighbor men departed
while he watched, leaning on his shovel
like a sergeant inspecting his recruits
or a god deciding who would live
to hear the kind of silence, so full
of sounds, that came to me
that morning as I lay abed, observing
the butter-like light at play

among curtains, secure
in the knowledge that my mother
was alive in the kitchen, my father
at work in the garage, the willow
tree out front swaying like an immense
dancer, skirts rippling as if to brush
all sorrow from the world,
and my dog asleep in its shade.

2. CLOVES

I look down from a bridge to where the sun
is a mysterious coin caught in the weir
of branches reflected in a fish pond.
Something swift and dark passes overhead,
a train announces that arrival and departure
are continuous. I have a handful of buttons
and a clove.

From a marsh somewhere beyond the trees,
frog song
and the blackbird's somewhat electronic
trill. Centuries go by like dobbins and flowers.

———

At age five the bridge, with its pleasant arc
and ornate railing, is my version of perfection,
that and Mrs. Mead laughing among dapples
of the apple boughs as she sits snapping beans
and tells me the story of a dance
in 1878 when Rolf Fredricksen drove up
in a carriage
with two dozen roses just for her.

Though I love the bridge, the happiness
of standing just at its highest point
above the pond with its iridescent fire
colored fish, I have come down to her
there at the edge of the orchard,
a ninety-two-year-old woman in a white shawl.

"He was a very beautiful boy," she says,
and gives each of us another clove, acrid
and wonderful.

We pop them into our mouths and sit
in the sun-drenched shade.

3. SPRING AND ALL

It was raining in the sunlight
of lost love I walked through, glove and cleats
slung over my shoulder,
blue ball cap set straight and low to keep the glare
from my reddened eyes.

The cop lurking in his prowler on the corner of Eighty-Second
    and Yamhill
watched me for signs of delinquency.
A salesman at the car lot three blocks down
decided not to bother. No one could help me
anyway, I supposed. All the songs said

when your girl stepped out on you it had to feel just
this way, as if someone had stolen the moon
and pissed in your ear.
Whatever you deserved was someone else's
idea, a flag without a pole.

I thought then death might be beautiful
as a car that would always start, or a fastball
with so much pop batters would freeze and weep
just thinking about it. I knew
I ought to be ashamed of feeling this way,

but I wasn't. It was good that everything mattered
so much, that I was king
of my own sadness, master of traipsing alone
through the neighborhoods of rain and light
toward a freedom from every judgment

but the strike zone and a half-blind umpire worried sick about one of his children.

4. NIGHT FISHING

Among the logjams and flotsam north of Brown's Landing,
    people from
the shacks and half-wrecked houseboats fished for channel cat
    and crappie.

Ragged loners and teenage boys came there as well and threw
    things in
or pulled them out or hid them in the flooded brushy inlets
    presumably

ignored by the constabulary. Sometimes night fishing there
    with lantern
and a box of horrible rum-soaked crooks, dark forms rose
    near us

like submarines listening, mystified Germans, perhaps,
    trapped there since the war
and wondering if they should kill us or simply steal our catfish
    and cigars.

We never knew. We reached out with our flashlights and found
    the river
meditative, clueless, and unitary as the sky where the huge
    chandelier

of the universe turned, and Sputnik scored its winking caveat:
    "There's more
up here than Heaven, boys. Breathe deep." And so we did,
    while

below us, we were certain, more than fish circled and tugged
　　at our lines
with dark or bright mouths, with the hunger of all unknown
　　things.

5. THE VISIT

My father enters with such human care,
I nearly forget
he's been dead for twenty years.

Beside that brass lamp by the door
he stops to look at me, at this room
overflowing with books and other forms
of precious junk I've lugged
through all the jobs and cities, all
the half beginnings of my time on earth.

I think he supposes us intimate
strangers now, that nothing could explain us,
much less the happiness we feel in this
late-night communion
miles and miles from where our days together
made their little footprints in the dust.

I don't dare to speak
lest I frighten the moment
away. For his part, he simply stands inside
that calm he carried
everywhere, and has no need to tell me why
he's come.

Certainly he's here to spill no secrets
about death, no news concerning the joys
and perils of the afterlife
or the meaning of it all.

He has brought only himself, looking
a little tired, but happy, and vaguely expectant, as though

we had arranged to go fishing
and now it's time.

6. TO THE UNDINE CHILD

I sat down to tell you why
the wren hates the badger
but forgot you were no longer
here, wherever
here is—we simply climb witless
into its aching arms. I suppose

when you step each night
from the sea
the water god looks at his watch
and shakes his huge and stringy head.
I suppose you come back for a bit
of the birdsong breeze
brightening your skin again.

Maybe there's a meadow somewhere
in your soul. But all day
driving words like nails, I don't
know which door to open for you, which
path summons the miraculous
skylark of the drowned risen
incorruptible and shining like the horrible
horrible sea
from which I do not know how
to keep you.

SET FREE OF THE PROBABLE

Out on the edge of the moon
my old cat, Al, is prancing again, just as
he did in life, his soul insisting the dumb
shrubs in our yard are full of birds, surely,
that rosy fascinations spring
from every shallow footprint in the grass.
I can hear him singing still, sweet

and perversely curious, luring the fat raccoon
from behind the garage.

He has been dead nine hours
and the beautiful emptiness in me is his
exact shape set free of the probable.
How could I not see him flying, beyond all
suffering and hope, grooming himself, leaving
this message where only those of us doomed
by love could find it?

A TRILLIUM FOR JAMES WRIGHT ON
THE ANNIVERSARY OF HIS PASSING

I see you in lamplit cold Ohio,
snow drinking your footprints as you pass.
Black branches of the wind
sound like a thousand blind men
tapping on an icy street, just
as I tap these keys to find you
who died long years ago in a country still
almost in love with distances and furrows,
its tinhorn jalopy-like goodwill
strolling down Main, making
the best of itself.

Today the country has a ruined face,
like that girl you wrote of,
and cannot blunt the meannesses that sneer
and dance away from every form of grace.
Today we need you and you're gone
into "the unbelievable silk of spring"
that does not know us
and comforts only the crows of winter dead
on their broken shore.

The fault is yours for none of this,
old friendly shadow lingering here.

So I whistle you for luck
and step down to the river in the dark
where little ripples signal to the moon,
their brother in loneliness and light,
that two are gathered here to walk and sing of them
beyond the grave in blossom
and the country's pain, beyond all scars and dying
and the night, that blackened blue
into which all of us are gone, some way
or other, looking for you.

TWO SOLITUDES

—for Ray

I.

Evening: a fire of blue crows bent
toward their perfect distribution. Suppose
I wander from the rose tent
of the faithful, give up
singing. I could carve myself
anew and go on with my allocution, angels

or not. I could circle back like Jesus
in a powerboat, plucking himself from the sea
after a long walk.

Blasphemy, of course.
But if there's a window out here
I hand it my sleeve, my fog of breath,
and look through, praying again.
Why not. Day is done and I offer myself
words, shells, their pink sinless hearts.

II.

Fly by night? Additionally perhaps
a screw loose.
But what sense is there for ironing
out? Only the wind's ripped coat, your father's
sore quietude after harvest, the love that
cannot set down its tools.

Too much for any of us, since we are
so far from home, since we are
our own home now, beaten
a bit, infused with cinders and smoke
of a thousand years. Since it is
evening.

HOMECOMING

I put on my good black shoes, my shirt
of grey softness that reminds me of luck,

and the blue hat given me
by a child who left

this earth that even her shadow
made so beautiful.

And then, well, I set out
down the clamor of roads

and, almost by accident, onto paths
through dense apothecaries of evergreen and fern

and finally to meadow and orchard
risen from the dead into a contentment

that did not know me
and wouldn't take my money or my name.

Did I not see I was the same no one
who had lived there always

and could never return?
Did I not perceive the multitudes

waving their arms like wind to be known again
and gathered like pieces of a god?

How many many years, how much spent blood,
to unpilgrim ourselves, to stand before an empty house

glistening with the grief of a happy life.

ACKNOWLEDGMENTS

Alaska Quarterly Review: "The Visit"

Basalt: "Wordsworth," "As He Is," "Dark Night: Newport 4:00 A.M.," "St. Theresa Returns," "God Bless the Child," "Dante's Crossing," "Canticle for Gilgamesh," "Ovid Still"

The Bellingham Review: "Ingmar Bergman Postcard," "It's Difficult to Mean One's Words"

Cloudbank: "When We Were Very Young"

Field: "Another Crossing," "Turnpike and Flow," "Winter Companion," "Historical Perspective," "To the Undine Child"

Fifth Wednesday: "The Giant Causes the Apocalypse"

5 Trope: "Surveillance," "Message," "To the Undine Child"

The Gettysburg Review: "More or Less," "Spring and All," "Graham Greene," "Paradise Null," "End," "A Doll's House"

Glassworks: "Open Any Door"

The Hampton-Sydney Review: "Before Genesis"

Hubbub: "Our Prayers Are Answered"

Image: "Cloudless," "Lacrimae Rerum," "In Consequence"

The Kerf: "Cloves"

Lake Effect: "Knowledge," "The End of Heracleitus"

Miramar: "Somewhere Behind the Blank Screens," "Cloud of Unknowing," "Two Solitudes," "Underway," "Set Free of the Probable," "A So-Called Respite"

Poetry International: "Creation," "Homecoming"

Poetry Northwest: "Kierkegaard's Instant," "Glimpsed in Passing" (as "Shutter")

Rock and Sling: "A Trillium for James Wright on the Anniversary of His Passing"

Sou'wester: "The Last Bus"

The Swamp: "Seasons of Love and Water," "Home on the Range; or Mortality and the Persistent Failure to Arrive"

Terminus: "Beyond Theology the Soul," "Simple Operation"

Terrain: "Night Fishing," "Implicit"

"The Better Part of Valor" appeared in *Poets Unite*, edited by Emily Gwinn and Michael Schein (Yakima, WA: Moon Cave Press, 2016).

"A So-Called Respite" appeared in *WA 129*, edited by Tod Marshall (Spokane, WA: Sage Hill Press, 2017).

"The End of Heracleitus" appeared as a broadside published in 2014 by North River Books, Marshfield Hills, Massachusetts.

The author wishes to express his gratitude to the editors of the publications listed above, and to extend special thanks to Melissa Kwasny, Christopher Buckley, David Axelrod, and Lex Runciman for their generous and intelligent commentary on the poems in this collection and, as always, for their friendship.

ABOUT THE AUTHOR

Born in Portland, Oregon, Christopher Howell attended Pacific Lutheran and Oregon State Universities, and holds graduate degrees from Portland State University and the University of Massachusetts. He is author of twelve collections of poems, including *Love's Last Number, Gaze,* and *Dreamless and Possible: Poems New and Selected* (University of Washington Press, 2010). He has received the Washington State Governor's Award, the Washington State Book Award, two National Endowment Fellowships, two fellowships from Artist Trust, the Vachel Lindsey and Helen Bullis Prizes, and a number of other fellowships and awards. His work has made three appearances in the annual *Pushcart Prize* collection and may be found in many journals and anthologies. A military journalist during the Vietnam War, since 1975 he has been director and principle editor for Lynx House Press and is now also director for Willow Springs Books. He lives in Spokane, where he is a member of Eastern Washington University's master of fine arts faculty.